Dogs and Cats

and

Hear Much, Much More!

By Janet Marlow, M.A.

For kids ages 7-12

ISBN: 978-1-4276-5038-2

Library of Congress Control Number: 2010938890

To the Parents

This book is written so that your child will understand how dogs and cats relate to the world through their acute sense of hearing. Hearing is an important sense that affects pet behavior. Children also have acute hearing. By learning about their pet in this way, your child will also learn to be aware of their own hearing sense and how it affects them in their daily lives.

In nature, animals use their acute hearing for survival. Reaction to sound is a part of pet behavior in the home, as a family member. This is most obvious when your dog or cat runs to the kitchen at the first sound of the treat jar opening! Teaching children how the science of sound affects their own environment, as well as their pet's living space, is one of the goals of this book. Better understanding of animals enhances empathy, responsibility and care for another being; therefore opening the hearts of children in the most natural way.

Dedicated to

The next generation -
Stewards of our Earth's animals.

Dogs and Cats Hear Much, Much More! - Janet Marlow

A Note from Janet Marlow

Because of a lifetime of being a musician and a researcher, I have been passionate in learning about sound and the joy of music. Through the field of neuro-science we are seeing that human behavior is profoundly affected by music. Everywhere we go music can be heard in the environment. We hear music in stores, medical offices and restaurants. Music is a mood changing experience. Listening to music elicits a physical and emotional response from people. Today, research studies show that music has a positive effect on animal behavior, as well as humans. As we live more closely with our pets, we are learning that there are significant commonalities between humans and animals. While your child is learning about the responsibility of how to care for their pet, the information in this book will help your child learn about science, inventors, language communication and the power of music.

Rags is my wonderful terrier companion. Adopting him has been one of the great joys of my life. I would like to thank Sandy VanAmburg for illustrating the essence of his happy character, in order to share with the children reading this book.

Thank you to the following special people whose thoughts, comments and directions helped me formulate this book: Sandy VanAmburg whose artistic characterizations are a joy to feature, Jim VanAmburg whose keen eye is to be admired, Natalie Pope Boyce, encouraging and kind, author of the Magic Tree House Research Guide, Melissa Brodeur, my 11 year old friend who helped edit this book from her youthful insights, Will Osborne, a dear and brilliant friend, Mary Pope Osborne, author of the Magic Tree House® series, whose friendship and place as a children's author worldwide is truly our National treasure, Elena Mannes, Emmy Award winning producer, whose film documentary, *The Music Instinct* inspired me to continue to look deeper into the power of music and to my sons, Ross and Colin, whose intelligence and dialogues accompanied me during the writing process. One more important thank you! To all the students I have taught, who mirrored the principle that knowledge is a dialogue to be shared, no matter what the subject and no matter what the age.

x   Dogs and Cats Hear Much, Much More! - Janet Marlow

Contents

Dogs and Cats Hear Much, Much More! - Janet Marlow

CHAPTER 1

WHAT IS SOUND?

Air is all around you. It is invisible. Even though you can't see air, it is filled with a lot of activity. This activity is called "sound."

Sounds that your ears hear can come from a rumbling truck passing by, a rushing river after a rain, squeaks from a bicycle brake, birds chirping in the trees, a speedy airplane, cracks of lightning during a thunderstorm, a dog barking, a door slamming and dry leaves crunching under your sneaker. These are sounds that you *can* hear. There are also sounds, that exist in the air, that you *cannot* hear.

Science is the way that people measure things that we can hear and not hear. There are words that scientists use to measure sounds that we *cannot* hear. Sound can go so high and so low that only measuring machines can show us that they exist.

These words are: decibel, frequency and sound waves.

These scientific words also relate to music.

These words are: volume, pitch and rhythm.

SCIENCE		MUSIC
DECIBEL	=	VOLUME
FREQUENCY	=	PITCH
SOUND WAVE	=	RHYTHM

Rags says, "Let's learn about the word decibel"!

Decibel means a unit of sound measured as volume; very soft to very loud!

The measurement of decibels was invented by Alexander Graham Bell (1847-1922) who was also the inventor of the first telephone. The first part of the word **deci**bel means ten. - (10 cycles of sound) - The second half of the word is "bel" named after Mr. Bell. Altogether the word becomes decibel.

Here are sounds that we *can* hear every day, measured in decibels. -(dB) -

Near total silence - 0 dB
A whisper - 15 dB
Normal conversation - 60 dB
A lawnmower - 90 dB
A car horn - 110 dB
A rock concert or a jet engine - 120 dB
An explosion - 150 dB

Felice says, "Let's learn about the word frequency"!

A German physicist by the name of Heinrich **Hertz** (1857-1894), discovered how to measure sound as pitch. This is called a "frequency". A frequency can be a very high pitch, all the way down to a very low pitch. Guess what? They named a word after him also, just like Mr. Bell (Deci**Bel**). We use the last two letters in his name **Hertz** and turn it into **Hz** to describe a frequency. A Hertz (Hz) is a unit of frequency or one cycle of sound per second.

Scientists can also measure how different animals hear in frequencies (Hz).

A bat can hear the sound of a mosquito's wing flying far away in the air. A bat's ears can hear from very low to very high frequencies.

Bat hearing in frequencies is: 2,000 Hz to 110,000 Hz.

Your ears can hear from 20 Hz to 20,000 Hz! This is just right for you and me but bats hear much, much more.

A porpoise hears and communicates with another porpoise from many, many miles away, deep in the ocean. A porpoise can hear frequencies from 75 Hz to 150,000 Hz. That is higher than a bat! Water carries sound even faster and longer distances than through the air.

Bats and porpoises are *echo locating* animals. That means that they send sounds out into the air or water and listen for the echoes that bounce back from the other animal. That is incredible!

Elephants can hear extremely low sounds. An elephant can hear frequencies from: 16 Hz to 12,000 Hz. - Much, much lower than bat hearing and human hearing. Elephants can make sounds that we can hear and not hear. You may have heard an elephant at the Zoo or on TV as they lift their trunks to make a loud trumpet like call. When an elephant talks to another elephant, they also make sounds in very low frequencies. These sounds are so low that if you were standing next to an elephant, you could not hear these low frequencies or sounds. That is because these sounds are below human hearing. Elephants are some of our Earth's special animals.

Rags wants you to know...

A scientist by the name of Katy Payne was the first person to discover that elephants hear and communicate in **infrasonic** frequencies or below 20Hz. Really, really, really low pitches!

Just like the title of this book, *Dogs and Cats Hear Much, Much More!* Dogs and cats can hear very high and very low frequencies. They hear much more than humans do! The fact is that dogs hear twice as much and cats hear three times as much as humans. Just like bats and elephants, dogs and cats hear sounds in the air that we cannot hear. Isn't that amazing?

Felice says, "Let's learn about sound waves"!

Do you know the fun of throwing a pebble into the water? First, you see a circle that starts from the center where the pebble dropped into the water and then the circles of waves go further away from the center. This is what sound waves look like as they get pushed into the air. Sound waves are like ripples that move sound out into the air and into our ears as sound.

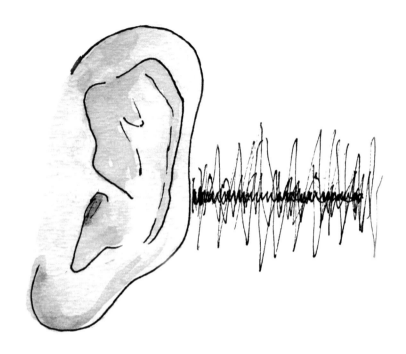

Frequencies, decibels and sound waves are everywhere, even in our houses. There are humming tones from a light in the ceiling, high pitches from a refrigerator and rumblings from a furnace and whirring air fans in a computer. All of these things make sounds that are sent out into the air of your home. If you lean your ear close to the refrigerator door, you will hear many sounds or frequencies.

Here are some common appliances that make sounds in your house.

Radio and Television

When you tune in to your favorite radio or television show, you are actually tuning the frequencies measured in **kilohertz (kHz).**

Computers

The speed of a computer is measured in **megahertz (MHz) and gigahertz (GHz).**

Microwave ovens are measured in **terahertz (THz).**

As you listen to all the sounds in your house, your two ears will be hearing decibels (dB), frequencies (Hz) and sound waves. You're awesome!

Chapter 2

Sounds Good To Me!

Imagine that you are standing in the center of a big grassy field in a park. The sounds that you can hear come from all around you in a circle. You can hear birds in the trees, the wind against your ears, the crunch of your foot on a dirt road, the plane flying above and cars on a nearby road.

Try this exercise just where you are. Take your hands and put them behind each ear, pushing your ears forward. You will hear all the sounds around you louder and more clearly. Have you ever seen your dog or cat do this when they want to listen carefully to a sound? They do this by bringing their ear muscles forward to capture the sound that they are listening to. This makes the sound louder or more intense.

Because you are a young person, your hearing is really good or another word is "acute". That means that you can hear very high and very low sounds (Hz) and very soft and very loud (dB) sounds. As people get older, they can't hear as well as a young person can hear. Have you ever placed your hands over your ears to muffle a harmful sound like a loud crash or crack of lightning? That is your instinct to protect your ears from the pressure of the sound on your eardrum. Just like your hand bouncing off a musical drum, sounds bounce from your eardrum.

Hearing is an important sense just like touch, taste, sight and smell. Hearing helps us to listen and learn, to be able to talk and also to enjoy music. Your ears hear *24* hours a day. Even when you are asleep!

Rags says, "Let's learn about language"!

Hearing and speaking go together. You have to hear a sound to know how to make a sound. Scientists believe that the language of early mankind started as music-like-singing for communication.

Your dog or cat speaks in a language as well! You can know exactly what your pet wants by the sounds they make, like purring, meows, barking, whines and whimpers. Communicating through sound is the way that humans and animals relate to each other.

CHAPTER 3

DOGS' EARS, BIG AND SMALL

Dogs (canines) hear twice as much sound as you do! This helps dogs survive in nature. Have you seen your dog react to a loud thunderstorm by running to hide? These sounds are very strong in a dog's ear. A dog also *feels* the vibration of a sound in their body, especially through their paws, on the ground. Dogs will often shake and shiver nervously from hearing and feeling a thunderstorm. This is because they hear sound at a very strong level.

Have you ever watched your dog run to the window barking at something outside but, when you look, you can't see or hear anything? That is because your dog is hearing something that your human hearing is not picking up. Dogs can also hear sounds at 1/600 of a second. That is faster than saying the word "second" as fast as you can!

The shape and size of a dog's ear also helps them to hear sounds.

Here are some breeds of dogs with different ear shapes and sizes. Do you see your dog in this picture?

Hound dogs have ears that go almost to the ground. Hunting by their sense of smell is their job or purpose. Long ears, close to their head, helps to keep the smell very strong in their noses, as they follow the trail of the scent.

German Shepherds have ears that go straight up. This breed of dog can be trained to hear the most distant of sounds. German Shepherds are often trained to be rescue dogs because they have excellent hearing.

The shape of a dog's ears tells us what job the dog is meant to do. Whether your dog is big or small, their ears are an important part of how they live their lives.

Dogs understand and react to sound differently than you do. When you hear most sounds like a car or a knock on the door, you think "what is that?" and then you react by moving away or towards the sound. When a dog hears an unfamiliar sound, it does not think but reacts by barking, sniffing in the air or running away. These are good reactions by your dog because, out in the wild, quick reactions through hearing are necessary to survive.

In your home, even though your dog knows that he or she is safe and loved, your dog still has this strong instinct to react to sound. Because your dog is part of your family, your dog will bark to protect and alert you. Dogs are listening and reacting to sound all day long, even if they look asleep. A dog can go from a deep sleep to standing and barking, in a split second, alerting the household that there is someone coming to the door.

When you spend time with your dog, watch their ears carefully. Try to hear what they are hearing. You can be a scientist, learning about sound, just by watching your dog's ears!

Dogs and Cats Hear Much, Much More! - Janet Marlow

CHAPTER 4

CATS' EARS, MOUSE SQUEAKS

Cats (felines) hear three times more than you do. This makes cats extremely sensitive to sound. Hearing is one of the most important senses that cats depend on for survival in nature. Cats hear higher sounds and lower sounds than dogs. Ready for the numbers?

45 Hz to 64,000 Hz.

Here is a dog's hearing range so that you can see how much lower and how much higher cats can hear than dogs!

Dogs 67 Hz to 45,000 Hz

Cats 45 Hz to 64,000 Hz

You can experiment with your cat's hearing ability by talking in a very high voice to see their reaction. A cat likes to hear high tones because these pitches are comfortable for them to hear. Cats are good mice hunters because they can hear the high squeaks and tiny movements that mice produce. A mouse can also hear the cat approaching because they can hear frequencies from 1,000 Hz to 91,000 Hz. More than a cat can hear!

Try this experiment with your cat! Clap your hands together once, away from your cat's ears and watch his or her head turn to you quickly, or perhaps it may run away. Observing how your cat responds to sound is a good way to understand your furry friends, through their amazing sense of hearing.

Most cat breeds have upright ears, which make responding to sound easy. Cats also have extra ear muscles. A cat can easily turn their ears for surround sound-like hearing. Watching your cat's ears is the best way for you to know what your cat is hearing and feeling.

Do you see your breed of cat in this picture?

Felice says, "Let's compare human and animal hearing"!

Dogs and Cats Hear Much, Much More! - Janet Marlow

Chart of human, dog, cat and horse hearing.

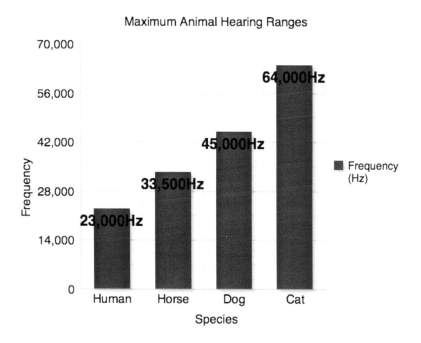

Maximum Animal Hearing Ranges

Can you see on the chart that horses and humans have the closest hearing range by the numbers shown? As a matter of fact, the horse has the closest hearing range to a human than any other mammal on the planet. Horses have been the transportation for humans for thousands of years until the invention of the train, and then the car. Isn't that fascinating to think about?

Dogs and cats have been part of peoples' lives for thousands of years as well. Dogs and cats have been sculpted by artists as statues in ancient Egypt and painted by artists in portraits of royal Kings and Queens, with their pets sitting by their side. Animals are an important part of human history.

Chapter 5

It's Music To Our Ears!

Music is everywhere! You can hear music in the supermarket, on your school bus, in your classroom, at the doctor's office and at the shopping mall. Music makes us happy, thoughtful and feel like dancing.

Dogs and cats love music too! Dogs and cats react in a positive way to music because it is made up of sounds that they hear in nature, such as pitch, tone and volume. Dog barks and cat meows are sounds in pitch, tone and volume.

If a dog or cat likes the music you are playing, they will curl up and rest. If there are strong vibrations from a drum roll coming from your music system, a dog or cat will flee (run away) from the room. Loud sounds and high pitches can feel like pressure in a pet's ear. Dogs and cats like to rest all day long. Music is a way to help them feel in balance and happy.

In this book, you have learned that your pet is sensitive to sounds. Dogs and cats and especially puppies and kittens don't like to be left alone when parents have to go to work and kids go to school. This makes them feel nervous because the house does not have the comfort of voices and the activity of their family. In pet behavior terms we call this "separation anxiety." When your pet is home alone, leave music playing all day long. Music will fill the air with a sense of calm and comfort. Play soothing, soft music. When you return home, your pet will be happy and ready for play time with you!

Music can also be helpful to calm behavior in your dog or cat at a visit to the veterinarian's office, while traveling in the car, during thunderstorms, while being groomed, at the kennel or when your pet is keeping you company while you do your homework.

Dogs and Cats Hear Much, Much More! - Janet Marlow

CHAPTER 6

AN ANIMAL GAME

Arrange the following animals by where they live on the Earth.

Water, Land and Trees

Below you see the name of the animal on the left column and the hearing range by frequencies on the right column. Write on a piece of paper which animal lives in the water, on land or in the trees.

Species	Approximate Range (Hz)
Human	64-23,000
Dog	67-45,000
Cat	45-64,000
Cow	23-35,000
Horse	55-33,500
Sheep	100-30,000
Rabbit	360-42,000
Rat	200-76,000
Mouse	1,000-91,000
Gerbil	100-60,000
Guinea pig	54-50,000
Hedgehog	250-45,000
Raccoon	100-40,000
Ferret	16-44,000
Opossum	500-64,000
Chinchilla	90-22,800
Bat	2,000-110,000
Beluga whale	1,000-123,000
Elephant	16-12,000
Porpoise	75-150,000
Bullfrog	100-3,000
Tree frog	50-4,000
Canary	250-8,000
Parakeet	200-8,500
Cockatiel	250-8,000
Owl	200-12,000
Chicken	125-2,000
Cockatiel	250-8,000

Which animal hears the highest frequency?

Which animal hears the lowest frequency?

Which animals hear the closest to a human? Answers in back of book!

Dogs and Cats Hear Much, Much More! - Janet Marlow

Answers to The Animal Game!

Water

1. Beluga Whale
2. Porpoise
3. Bullfrog

Land

1. Chicken
2. Bullfrog
3. Human
4. Dog
5. Cat
6. Elephant
7. Raccoon
8. Ferret
9. Hedgehog
10. Horse
11. Cow
12. Sheep
13. Rabbit
14. Rat
15. Mouse
16. Gerbil
17. Guinea Pig
18. Chinchilla

Trees

1. Tree Frog
2. Cockatiel
3. Parakeet
4. Owl
5. Bat

Dogs and Cats Hear Much, Much More! - Janet Marlow

Research References

Katharine Boynton Payne (born 1937) is a researcher in the Bio-acoustics' Research Program at the Laboratory of Ornithology at Cornell University. In 1999, she founded the lab's Elephant Listening Project.

In an issue of the *Journal of the American Medical Association,* researchers from the Brigham and Women's Hospital in Boston analyzed federal data collected from national yearly surveys of the health of American citizens. Researchers say this means that 1 in 5 adolescents now suffers some sort of hearing impairment. - August 2010

Signing, Singing, Speaking: How Language Evolved by JON HAMILTON, NPR - August 2010

The Music Instinct DVD, Elena Mannes, Director - THE MUSIC INSTINCT: SCIENCE AND SONG provides a ground-breaking exploration into how and why the human organism and the whole ebb and flow of the cosmos is moved by the undeniable effect of music. This follows visionary researchers and accomplished musicians to the crossroads of science and culture in search of answers to music' s deep mysteries. Featuring: Bobby McFerrin & Dr. Daniel Levitin, author of This is Your Brain on Music.

Heffner, H. E. and Heffner, R. S. (2007). Hearing ranges of laboratory animals.

Journal of the American Association for Laboratory Animal Science, **46**, 11-13.

Heffner, H. E., & Heffner, R. S. (1992). Auditory perception. In C. Phillips and D. Piggins (Eds.), Farm Animals and the Environment. (pp.159-184). Wallingford UK: CAB International.

Heffner, H. E. (1998). Auditory awareness in animals. Applied Animal Behavior Science, **57**, 259-268.

Johnson, H. Taylor (2006) The Art of Sound, Taylor Hohendahl Engineering, Jan. 2006 www.theaudio.com

Masteron, B. and Diamond, I.T. (1973) Hearing: Central Neural Mechanisms. (In: Carterette, E.C. and Friedman, M.P. 9eds) Handbook of Perception, vol. 3 Biology of Perceptual Systems. Academic Press, New York, pp.407-448.

Mattila, A.S. and Wirtz, J. (2001), Congruency of Scent and Music as a driver of In-Store Evaluations and Behavior, In: Journal of Retailing **77**, pp. 273-289.

Wolfe, J. (2007) What is a decibel? The University of New South Wales, Sydney, Australia, Music Acoustics, www.phys.unsw.edu.au.

Google reference June 3, 2003 Article George M. Strain Professor of NeuroscienceComparative Biomedical SciencesSchool ofVeterinary Medicine Louisiana State University

RR Fay. 1988. Hearing in Vertebrates: a Psychophysics Data book. Hill-Fay Associates, Winnetka IL.

D Warfield. 1973. The study of hearing in animals. In: W Gay, ed., Methods of Animal Experimentation, IV. Academic Press, London, pp 43-143.

HE Heffner. 1983. Hearing in large and small dogs: Absolute thresholds and sizes of the tympanic membrane. Behav Neurosci 97:310-318.

Janet Marlow, 2008, Zen Dog: Music and Massage for a Stress Free Pet Barnes & Noble, Metro Books.

About the Author

Janet Marlow is an international expert in the pet field, as an author, researcher and composer. Her Relaxation Music for Dogs, Cats and Horses has proven a success of putting animals at ease— acoustically and scientifically. Her innovative approach for animals has been featured on Animal Planet, Everyday with Rachel Ray, Women's World, WNPR, Dog Fancy, Modern Dog and in Animal Wellness Magazines. In March 2009, Barnes & Noble released her book and box kit *Zen Dog: Music and Massage for a Stress Free Pet*. This unique kit helps dog owners tap into the power of music and gentle massage, to improve their dog's mental and physical well being.

Her research and music is recognized by the Animal Behavior Society, Green Chimneys' Childrens' Animal Assisted Education Service, Pet Sitters International, the New York-Presbyterian Weill Cornell Medical

Center, Animal Specialty Center Hospitals, the Pony Farm Therapeutic Program, animal shelters and rescue organizations. Janet Marlow gives workshops and book talks on pet hearing of dogs, cats and horses for adults and children and appears frequently at Barnes & Noble Bookstores for Zen Dog. She is a member of The Authors' Guild and the American Pet Product Manufacturers' Association. Janet Marlow is co-founder of Pet Acoustics Incorporated. The company mission *"is dedicated to creating a sound world for animals and their people".*

Janet Marlow's passion, for music and the understanding of the effects of this language on humans and animals, comes from a lifetime of being a musician, teacher, concert performer and animal lover. She is internationally acclaimed for her concerts, recordings and compositions in classical and jazz. Janet is one of the leading masters and players of the ten-string guitar and she is the founder and director of the International Ten String Guitar Society and Festivals. Her singing and playing are featured in Woody Allen's movie "Celebrity" and she played a ten-string guitar on the score of the award winning Sun Dance Film Festival "Swimmers". Her performances have taken her around the world, which include venues such as Lincoln Center, Texaco Jazz Festival, Festival Estival De Paris, Quick Center for the Arts, The Apollo, Carnegie Hall and the Blue Note in NY. Write to Janet Marlow at janetmarlow@petacoustics.com

About the Illustrator

Sandy VanAmburg is a full time elementary art teacher in Connecticut and she holds a masters degree in art education. Her paintings were included in the CCSU Graduate Exhibition sponsored by the Art League of New Britain, featuring the work of the graduate students from Central Connecticut State University. "A Painter's Joyful Expression", was held at the 550 Gallery, Bethlehem, CT, an exhibition in partial fulfillment of the requirements for the degree of Masters in Art Education at Central Connecticut State University. Sandy received the teacher of the year award from her elementary school in 2007.

She has owned and operated an extensive crafts' business, "The Crafty Bird". Her products were featured in many retail locations throughout New England.

Her latest endeavor is a line of illustrations she calls 'naminals', part name, part animal and all fun. She has recently launched her website www.naminals.org

and offers prints and items for sale especially for the gift and holiday markets.

A Letter from Rags and Felice

Dear Friends,

We'd love to hear from you!

Please write to us if you'd like to share an adventure or a funny story about you and your pet. We are collecting, kids with pets' stories, for our next book.

Our address is:

Pet Acoustics Kids
18 Titus Road
PO Box 26
Washington Depot, CT 06794

Or send us your story in an email: bark@petacoustics.com

Paws and Purrs,
Rags and Felice

Dogs and Cats Hear Much, Much More! - Janet Marlow

About Pet Acoustics

Pet Acoustics Inc. is a company dedicated to innovating products that bring balance and well being to animals and the people that share their lives with them.

For Pets and Kids

Relaxation Music for Pets and Kids CD and download

Relaxation Music for Pets and Kids is specifically designed to create a calming environment for pets and kids to enjoy together. Research shows that children exposed to relaxing music improve their mood.

Walking My Dog Kid Sized Leash made for kids to take the Lead! Walking My Dog kids' size leash™ is a solution to the problem of children having to wrap standard size leashes, meant for the adult hand and height. The shorter length will give a child better communication and control of their dog.

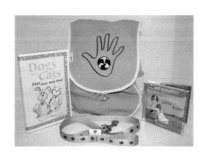

PetWorld Kids Back Pack : Includes Walking My dog Kid Sized Leash, Janet Marlow's book "Dogs and Cats Hear, Much Much More! Illustrations by Sandy VanAmburg, Relaxation Music for Pets and Kids CD, Eco -friendly, washable Back Pack to put it all in. Available on www. petacoustics.com

Other Products!

- CDs, Downloads and Apps

- Relaxation Music for Dogs and Cats

- Relaxation Music for My Dog and Me

- Relaxation Music for My Cat and Me

- Relaxation Music for Horses, for Equine Well Being

- Relaxation Music for the Holidays, for Pets and Pet Lovers

- Relaxation Music for Pets and Kids

- My Pet Speaker -The World's first sound system for the hearing sensitivities of dogs, cats and horses.

- Pet Acoustics App - iTunes

- Pet jingles App - iTunes

Janet Marlow's CDs and Download music for people on iTunes and Amazon

- Passion and Grace- classical

- Essence classical-Jazz

- Smooth Romance Jazz

- Latin Lover Latin jazz

- Good Company Jazz

- Janet Marlow Books

- Zen Dog: Music and Massage for a Stress Free Pet (Barnes & Noble).

- Guitar Practice: Tips and Techniques (Amazon.com)

- Playing the Ten String Guitar: An Approach Guide for Guitarists - Book and DVD (Amazon.com).

Visit our website for more information:

WWW.PETACOUSTICS.COM

Join our mailing list for events and
newsletters bark@petacoustics.com

Pet Acoustics Inc.
18 Titus Road/ PO Box 26
Washington Depot, Conn. 06794
1-866-228-3013 ext.3